# UNDERSTANDING BIBLE TEACHING

## The Nature of Man

### A Skevington Wood BA, Ph.D, FR.Hist.S

**Scripture Union**

47 Marylebone Lane, London W1 6AX

**Wm. B. Eerdmans**

225 Jefferson Avenue, Grand Rapids, Michigan

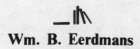

ISBN 0 85421 718 5 (Scripture Union)
ISBN 0 8028 1762 9 (Wm. B. Eerdmans)

Printed in Great Britain at the Benham Press
by William Clowes & Sons Limited, Colchester and Beccles

# General Introduction

There are many commentaries on the Biblical text and there are many systematic studies of Christian doctrine, but these studies are unique in that they comment on selected passages relating to the major teachings of the Bible. The comments are designed to bring out the doctrinal implications rather than to be a detailed verse by verse exposition, but writers have always attempted to work on the basis of sound exegetical principles. They have also aimed to write with a certain devotional warmth, and to demonstrate the contemporary relevance of the teaching.

These studies were originally designed as a daily Bible reading aid and formed part of Scripture Union's Bible Characters and Doctrines series. They can, of course, still be used in this way but experience has shown that they have a much wider use. They have a continued usefulness as a summary and exposition of Biblical teaching arranged thematically, and will serve as a guide to the major passages relating to a particular doctrine.

Writers have normally based their notes on the RSV text but readers will probably find that most modern versions are equally suitable. Many, too, have found them to be an excellent basis for group Bible study. Here the questions and themes for further study and discussion will prove particularly useful—although many individuals will also find them stimulating and refreshing.

# ONE

## God's Creature

### 1 : In the Image of God

**Genesis 1.26–2.9, 15–25**

The biblical and scientific accounts of man's origins agree in regarding him as the crown of creation. In Genesis both his affinity with the natural world and his superiority to it are equally stressed. He was fashioned from the dust and yet created in God's own image (2.7; 1.27). This combination supplies the key to man's complex nature. Scripture is sufficiently realistic to do justice to each of the elements involved.

The verb to create (bārā') stands for 'that divine creativity which is absolutely without analogy' (G. von Rad). It is included three times in one verse (1.27) as if to emphasize the uniqueness of man. The creative action is introduced, moreover, with a distinct divine resolution (1.26), indicating that God was here implicated more fully and closely than in His former works.

The specific feature in man which marks him off from the rest of creation is described as the image of God. 'Likeness' in 1.26 is simply an explanatory qualification. These complementary terms strongly assert that man in some way reflects his Creator. He shares the personhood of God. He is a self-conscious, rational, responsible being. Here lies his highest dignity (Gen. 9.6). In view of this fact, it is not surprising that there is widespread dissatisfaction among young people with the materialism (both theoretical and practical) of the present age. God made man with a spiritual dimension and this seeks fulfilment. The devil is not slow in supplying 'spiritual' alternatives to the gospel!

It is as one created in God's image that man can enter into dialogue with Him. This is what shows man to be a son of God, just as Seth was said to be after the image of Adam (Gen. 5.3). But the image cannot be maintained independ-

5

ently of the One whom it expresses. Hence the significance of 'breath' in 2.7. To be sure the same divine spirit conveys life to all animate creatures. Yet its function is to maintain what God has bestowed, and in the case of man this endowment is God's image.

As one who thus partakes of the divine nature (2 Pet. 1.4) man reproduces himself in procreation and exercises dominion over the earth and its creatures (Gen. 1.28). Like his Maker, man is both father and lord. Such was God's intention for him, and in such unsullied innocence and undisputed sovereignty he would presumably have continued had sin not intervened.

As we have seen, Gen. 2.7 reminds us that the physical differentiation between man and the animals is a matter of quality and not of substance. 'Breath of life' and 'living being' are not expressions confined to the human species (cf. Gen. 1.21, 24, 30; 2.19). Only in the case of man, however, is there a direct transfer of *rûah* by a special divine insufflation, and only in one like himself does he find an appropriate companion (2.18).

*A thought : I ought never to 'put on a pedestal' nor to underrate a creature of God, made in His image.*

## 2 : Man's Littleness and Greatness

### Psalm 8

The psalmist sees man first in relation to God and then in relation to the world of created things. When set in the sight of God he seems small indeed, but as over against the animal kingdom he is impressively great. Psa. 8 has been described as 'a poetic replica of the creation narrative of Genesis 1 so far as it refers to man' (J. Laidlaw). It is a meditation on the creation of man as envisaged retrospectively through the fall.

Man's comparative insignificance is apparent not only as he is measured against the majesty of God (1), but also as

6

he is placed in the context of the universe (3). He is no more than a speck of dust in the immensity of space. But this is to assess him purely in dimensional terms. Such a verdict overlooks the status God has bestowed on man. God has crowned him with glory and honour (5). Man, not nature, is the central theme of the Psalm. His God-given dignity is the real marvel of the universe.

'Wonders are many, and none is more wonderful than man,' wrote Sophocles in *Antigone*. But whereas Greek thought considered man's value to be inherent, the biblical revelation recognizes that it is solely of grace. Man's assets are what God has made over to him. That is why no realistic account of man can ignore his relationship to God. An age which denies God will inevitably fail to understand man. In Communism the interests of the individual are completely subordinate to those of the group. Man has no spiritual dimension. Religion is 'the opium of the people'. In some psychological theories man is little more than a very complex machine.

The true stature of man is measured by what God has made him. He falls only a little short of the angels (5, AV [as in the Septuagint and Vulgate], cf. Heb. 2.7f). In a strictly monotheistic context *Elóhîm* (the Hebrew word in v. 5) would appear to mean either God Himself (RSV, RV) or 'the inhabitants of heaven' (W. Eichrodt). The reference is to the image of God in man.

Man's dominion over the rest of creation is not seized by revolt, but received from God as a sacred trust (6). It is in stewardship that he controls the natural world (7 f.). In himself he is weak and insignificant. Under God alone can he claim to be the king of the earth. Recent interest in ecology, in conservation and pollution, testifies unconsciously to our responsibility to exercise this stewardship aright.

*Is my attitude towards the material things which are God's creation responsible and Christian?*

# 3 : The Miracle of Birth

## Psalm 139

The psalm is a paean of praise to God. It extols His omniscience (1–6), omnipresence (7–12), and omnipotence (13–18). Man is seen only in his dependence on his Creator. He is completely known to God. He has been subjected to the most searching scrutiny (3). Nothing is hidden from God. Nor can man hide himself. Even though he tries to escape, he cannot. The psalmist considers the various routes by which he might do so but decides that they are uniformly inadequate for the purpose.

He is led to dwell on the unlimited power of God. Psa. 8 illustrates the divine omnipotence by pointing to the creation of the universe (cf. also Psa. 104). Psa. 139 does so in terms of man's own origin. All that we now know about the process of human reproduction from conception to birth only serves to increase our wonder at the miracle. It is God who creates the inmost self, the essential personality, so as to claim possession of it (13). It is He who is responsible for the development of the embryo in the womb. Contemplation of the mystery can only call forth praise and gratitude (14). The bone structure of the human frame and the intricate interlacing of nerves, veins and muscles are all observed and indeed superintended by God. 'In the depths of the earth' (15) is used figuratively to describe 'the limbo of the womb' (JB). Elsewhere it refers to Sheol, the place of departed spirits (Psa. 63.9; 86.13). Here the womb is thought of as a dark underworld. We are not therefore to imagine some divine laboratory in the bowels of the earth.

'Unformed' (16) is literally 'rolled together' like a ball, and thus aptly applied to the foetus. Either all the days of the Psalmist's life are said to be entered in God's records, even before he was born (RSV, JB) or (more probably in the context of v. 16) all his limbs were similarly catalogued, and as they were fashioned 'not one of them was late in growing' (NEB). As he considers the incredible mystery of man's procreation, the Psalmist breaks out into renewed astonishment at the profundity and inexhaustibility of the divine wisdom (cf. Rom. 11.33). After announcing his hatred of the wicked who range themselves against such a gracious God (19–22), he returns to the theme of examination with which he began (23 f., cf. v. 1). Man's real well-being—my real well-being—consists in 'shunning every evil way, and walking in the good' (Charles Wesley).

# 4 : The Sanctity of Marriage

## Matthew 19.1–12

According to T. H. Robinson, 'this is the highest word ever uttered on marriage.' Our Lord's appeal under pressure from the Pharisees was not to the tradition of the elders but to Scripture. He referred His critics to their own final authority and cited Gen. 1.27 and 2.24 (4 f.).

The dispute focused on the interpretation of Deut. 24.1, with its sanctioning of divorce. There could be no question that according to the Jewish law divorce was allowed on certain grounds. But what are those grounds? What is meant by the qualification about a wife falling out of favour because of something shameful? The stricter school of Shammai took this to mean adultery. The more liberal followers of Hillel broadened it to include anything which displeased the husband—even to burning his food when cooking it.

If the Pharisees hoped to trap Jesus into taking sides on this issue they were disappointed. He cut right through the web of rabbinical casuistry to reach the heart of the matter as indicated by Scripture. God has created man and woman for each other to live in a monogamous union. They are bound together in such a way that they are no longer two but one (6). In view of this unique and exclusive relationship, any breach is unthinkable. It would amount to desecration in the undoing of God's work. Our Lord made no distinction between man and woman in this respect. His prohibition is equally binding on both, although in Jewish law only the man could take the initiative in divorce proceedings.

No place is thus left for the dissolution of a marriage. What then of the Mosaic regulation? Jesus explained that it was a concession to human obduracy. One of the effects of original sin was to petrify not only the feelings but the

9

understanding as well, with the result that man becomes virtually incapable of learning. This, however, was not so before the fall and it cannot therefore be argued that divorce was sanctioned from the beginning (8).

The exceptive clause (9) has been much debated in modern times. There are no grounds for excluding it from the text, as some have done. Although some commentators refer it to pre-marital fornication, it is more likely to apply to adultery. Adultery destroys the very foundations of marriage, although our Lord's alteration of 'command' to 'allow' (7 f.) will surely apply here also. Such divorce (with the possibility of remarriage?) would not be undertaken lightly by a Christian, but our Lord's teaching clearly permits it.

The disciples were clearly astonished at the high standard set by Jesus. They were tempted to wonder whether celibacy was perhaps preferable. But our Lord's teaching implies that marriage is normal for man, although some are called to renounce it for His sake.

## 5 : The Tyranny of the Tongue

### James 3.1–12

After a warning against ambitious over-eagerness to assume the role of a teacher in the church (1), James returns to a theme already introduced in 1.19, 26—namely, the need to control the tongue. He places this discipline in the context of ideal manhood in Christ. Although we are all liable to do wrong, since to err is human, nevertheless, maturity is a goal to be aimed at (2). We are meant to attain the purpose for which we were designed by our Creator and thus to find fulfilment. This involves the discipline not only of the tongue but indeed of the whole person. Such perfection is nothing less than the full realization of the divine likeness (9).

James provides a disturbing insight into our fallen nature as he vividly describes the tyranny of the tongue. He employs three successive illustrations of the truth he is seeking to bring out—that the tongue is the hinge on which man's entire personality turns (3 ff.). If a man can master his tongue, then he can master the rest, just as a rider controls a horse by means of a bit or a helmsman steers a ship even in a gale by means of a rudder. A raging forest fire may be started by a tiny spark and the tongue is similarly dangerous.

The last of these illustrations leads the apostle to enlarge on the menace of the tongue. He begins to mix his colours as he piles one analogy on another. The tongue is a microcosm of wickedness, a spreading stain of pollution, an untamed beast which prowls after its prey, and the venom of a deadly snake. But above all it is a fire—like flames running up all the spokes of a wheel from a burning axle. It sets alight the cycle of existence, fed from hell's own furnace (6 ff.).

James's reference to the image of God occurs in his allusion to the dual use of the tongue, both for blessings and curses. Such an anomaly ought not to be tolerated (10). The serious-ness of cursing lies in the fact that it is not only a sin against man but against God. To revile man is to do despite to the image in which he was created. From the Christian stand-point the only safeguard for human dignity is found in the divine Creatorhood.

It is interesting to notice that his language seems to imply that man (despite the fall) is still in some sense in the image of God (cf. 1 Cor. 11.7). Even at his most beastly he is still not a mere animal. God's love in our hearts stirs our com-passion towards the lost, and leads us to pray for their recreation in Christ.

## Questions and themes for study and discussion on Studies 1–5

1. In what ways is man akin to the animal creation and in what ways is he superior?

2. How is man's lordship over creation to be expressed today?

3. If a test-tube baby is eventually produced by science, would this invalidate the Christian view of birth?

4. Is the biblical insistence on the indissolubility of marriage intended to apply only to Christians?

5. What other New Testament passages contain warnings against the misuse of speech?

11

# TWO

## Fallen: The Genesis Record

### 6 : The Fall of Man

#### Genesis 3.1–7

So far we have been looking at man as he was in creation. Clearly this is not how he now is. How did he become otherwise? The Bible simply says that he fell. He lapsed from his original state of innocence. Nothing less than a major catastrophe affecting the whole of his personality is sufficient to account for man's present alienation and misery. Even modern philosophers like Heidegger resort to the categories of 'falling' and 'thrownness', though not, of course, with theological overtones.

The impulse to sin, according to the biblical account, came from outside man. Nothing in nature as given by God compelled him to fall. Yet it is equally evident that man is held responsible for his own defection. Even though the first human sin was induced by the tempter, it is regarded nevertheless as a wilful self-corruption on the part of its perpetrator.

The essence of the fall lay in disobedience. God's prohibition was sufficiently categorical (2.16 f.). The fatal stages which led up to the sinful act are traced in this chapter. Here is how man still succumbs. It began with doubting God's word (1). 'Did God say?'—according to F. Delitzsch 'a half-interrogatory, half-exclamatory expression of astonishment,' as if the serpent had brooded for a long time over the paradox and had eventually reached a reluctantly critical conclusion. When the woman had repudiated the serpent's distortion of the divine command—even over-correcting it with a proviso of her own (3)—the tempter threw aside insinuation and came out with a flat denial (4). Then he impugned God's motives by slyly suggesting that He wanted to keep man down lest His own prerogatives should be threatened. This unworthy charge was utterly groundless, for God's decree was designed only for man's good. Yet it contains the kernel of sin, which is the attempt to become like God (or 'gods', NEB). The titanism which aspired to usurp the Almighty power and wisdom brought about man's downfall. He wanted to become a law to himself. In his vaulting ambition he snatched at what belonged to God alone. Hence William of Sens confessed in Dorothy Sayer's play *The Zeal of Thy House* that he had been struck down by 'the eldest sin of all'—the pride that thinks it can play God.

Human eyes were now opened (5, 7) and immediately the spell of innocence was broken. Because he grasped what was forbidden, man has ever since experienced a 'longing which cannot be stilled' (E. Brunner).

*Meditation : The first sin was conceived in mistrust. What about my sins? Do they often begin there?*


# 7 : Results of the Fall

## Genesis 3.8–20

The immediate consequences of the fall are described in v. 7. It brought with it an awareness of sin's seriousness and a profoundly disturbing sense of shame. The feeling was at once the outcome of sin and a reaction against it.

In the interview with God that follows from v. 8 onwards an enquiry is conducted (9–13) and the sentences are pronounced (14–19). Man's communion with his Maker was impaired by his disobedience (8). It was not that God withdrew His presence. He appeared as before in the garden—the place of fellowship. But on hearing the rustle of His footsteps—His approach can only be indicated in such anthropomorphic terms—the guilty pair tried to conceal themselves. Avoidance of God was a further result of the fall. It is all the more tragic in that the One from whom they shrank was still reaching out to them in love. 'It was God their Creator who now, as God the Redeemer was seeking the lost' (Delitzsch).

God not only came but called (9). In grace He sought to elicit a response from man the sinner. Even when thus summoned the man multiplied excuses. The old confidence was broken. No wonder Luther commented that Adam was now totally changed to become another man. With the instinctive craftiness of an evil conscience he sidestepped responsibility by blaming his wife. The infection spread as the woman in turn blamed the serpent. Suddenly something was rotten in the state of Eden, as in Hamlet's Denmark. The knowledge of good and evil had spoiled man's original relationship with God. The key to man's fallen condition is to be found in v. 10: 'I was afraid.' As the psychologists confirm, fear invariably lies at the root of man's malaise.

The penalties imposed first on the serpent and then on Eve and Adam represent further consequences of the fall. The hostility between Satan and man brings in its train hatred, violence, oppression and strife (15). In the case of the woman sexual life is now accompanied by the labour pains of child-birth and the dominance of the male threatens to reduce her to subjugation. In the case of the man, work which had formerly been a delight now becomes a burden. For both, death waits at the end as 'a kind of sacrament of sin' (J. Denney).

*A Thought: In blaming another I often reveal that I am a Child of the Fall. Grace enables me to face up to moral reality.*

## 8: Paradise Lost

### Genesis 3.22–4.16

As soon as he became a sinner, man was ejected from the garden of Eden and excluded from the tree of life (3.23 f.). This banishment, enforced by the divine decree, was a logical necessity. Partaking of the tree symbolized eternal fellowship with God, for eternal life is knowing God (John 17.3). This was man's destiny at his creation. Probably, after a period of probation, he would be raised to the status of permanent sonship. But sin had now intervened. Man had chosen the way of death rather than the way of life. That decision was humanly speaking irrevocable. The return route is not merely difficult: it is altogether impossible to man, however much he may desire it. The flashing sword turns 'every way' in its comprehensive circular motion (24). If man is ever to find eternal life it will be by the sheer undeserved grace of God.

If Gen. 3 records the first human sin against God, Gen. 4 records the first sin of man against man. Of course, since man is made in the image of God, it is also a sin against God, for that is always the nature of sin (Psa. 51.4). When Cain's gift was rejected his reaction was one of resentment and dejection (5). God's probing question 'Why?' (cf. 'Where?' in Gen. 3.9) led to a solemn warning against the seduction of sin. In a vivid metaphor sin is depicted as a wild beast crouching in readiness to leap on its prey (7, cf. 1 Pet. 5.8). If Cain failed to master it, then it would master him. Sin is recognized as an objective force against man.

The murder of Abel appears as deliberate and cold-blooded. Cain invited his brother to go with him into the solitude of the open country where the crime would be unobserved (8). 'Human sin made a gigantic advance in this act' (Delitzsch). 'Where?' reappeared (cf. 3.9) as a social question (9). Cain's truculent reply suggests the hardening of sin.

The full weight of sin's offence is brought home as Cain cried out in his anguish (13). As von Rad puts it, he realized that a life far from God is a life He no longer protects. But the final word is with mercy as he received a promise of immunity from the blood avenger.

*Meditation: If God has graciously reconciled me to Himself, to what extent has this affected my relations with other people? (cf. Eph. 2.14-18; 1 John 2.9-11).*

# 9 : Universal Corruption
## Genesis 6.1–22

The enigmatic narrative about the origin of the Nephilim (1-4) is apparently introduced to account in part for the further corruption of mankind prior to the flood. As D.

Kidner suggests, however the passage is interpreted a new stage has been reached in the progress of evil, and man is seen to be beyond self-help.

A more emphatic and all-embracing assertion of human wickedness than is contained in v. 5 could scarcely be imagined. Its magnitude, its inwardness, its comprehensiveness, its continuity and its monotonous invariability are all alluded to. The effect on God of this pervasive depravity is indicated in v. 6. The purposes of grace seemed to be frustrated and God even began to regret that He had ever created man. He was so deeply grieved that He resolved on the destruction of the world (7). Here we see what sin means to God, and only as we realize how it appears in His sight do we begin to grasp the full extent of its enormity.

This devastating account of universal corruption is confirmed in vs. 11 f. The repetitions hammer home the grim fact. The earth was now filled with violence—arbitrary, anarchistic oppression and the elemental breach of law and order (11). The whole of mankind had deliberately involved itself in defection (12). Responsibility for this catastrophic state of affairs is firmly placed on man's own shoulders.

All this is strikingly, almost frighteningly, modern. Sin in society is not static, but is an ugly dynamic, a kind of active leaven affecting the whole lump. Societies do not move nearer righteousness but further away from it unless God brings a 'wind of change' towards Him by the Spirit of His grace in Christ. The unnatural sex (if the 'sons of God' are fallen angels, as many commentators think) and the plenitude of violence make us think of our own day.

There was, however, one exception to this otherwise unanimous indictment. Righteous Noah found favour in the sight of the God with whom he walked in fellowship and was chosen to be the pioneer of a new generation. But apart from Noah and his family no one was to be spared. God had determined to do away with the rest. 'End' (13) is a common term in later eschatology in connection with divine judgement. On the inclusiveness of the punishment depends the inclusiveness of the salvation foreshadowed by the ark.

*A Thought: If our intercession for such a world is to reach the heavenly Throne we need first to view the world* as *God does* and to acknowledge that we are ourselves *'debtors to mercy alone'*.

## Questions and themes for study and discussion on Studies 6-9

1. Evolutionary anthropologists appear to see only a 'rise' where the Bible speaks of a fall. What arguments can be advanced in support of the Christian view of man as fallen?

2. Consider Gen. 3.1–7 in the light of 1 Tim. 2.13 f. Is Paul really placing most of the blame on Eve, as is sometimes assumed?

3. How does Gen. 3.14–19 help us to understand the world in which we live?

4. Ponder the comments on Gen. 4 in Heb. 11.4 and 1 John 3.11 ff.

5. In what ways does the account of universal corruption before the flood find its counterpart in the modern world?

# THREE

## Fallen: In Psalms and Wisdom Literature

### 10 : Sin and Suffering

**Psalm 38**

This is the prayer of a repentant and chastened sinner. It is the third of the penitential psalms and designed to accompany a memorial offering (Lev. **2**.1–10; **24**.7). It is traditionally ascribed to David and although there is no direct hint as to the occasion, it is assumed that like Psa. **51** it has the king's adultery as its background. He is troubled in body, mind and soul. He is afflicted by a sickness which he recognizes as in some way associated with his sin. The reasons for his suffering are listed: 'because of thy indignation' (3), 'because of my sin' (3), 'because of my foolishness' (5).

There is no attempt to gloss over the seriousness of sin. The psalmist feels like a man in danger of drowning. His iniquities overwhelm him with the pressure of waves in flood (4). He sees his sin as folly (5b). He has played the fool, and his stupidity is all the more irresponsible because it is self-destructive. Sin has deprived him of joy: life is a misery and he goes about in black like one bereaved (6). He is 'all battered and benumbed' (NEB) and the wild surging of his heart makes him growl like a lion in pain (8). What sin pays out is death (Rom. **6**.23) and the distribution begins even in life. Sin, suffering and wrath are all inter-related, although suffering may not necessarily be the result of a man's own wrongdoing.

The psalm contains three distinct appeals to God's mercy (1, 9, 15.). The recognition that chastisement is inflicted by God brings with it the assurance that it will not prove too hard to bear and that relief and restoration will follow. God's arrows have been aimed at the psalmist and God's hand has pressed down heavily on him (2). His plight is known to the Lord who hears his sighs (9). Hence he can

18

confidently commit his cause to God and fix his hope on Him (15). The Lord will answer with forgiveness.

The psalmist concludes with a frank confession. His foot often slips (16). He is always liable to fall headlong, for he is incapable of standing firm in his own strength. He cannot escape from the consciousness of his guilt: godly sorrow for sin is his constant companion. He freely admits his iniquity and makes no secret of it. His is the repentance of faith which despairs of itself but not of God.

What can we learn from all this? Job's comforters were wrong when they dealt with Job on the assumption that his sickness was the result of some awful and specific sin in his own life. Nevertheless, the modern doctor and psychiatrist have plenty of experience of ailments which have their source in the sufferer's own wrongdoing. To any such this psalm presents a case to face reality—the ugly reality of sin and the glorious reality of the forgiveness God offers to the truly penitent. In such circumstances we can identify ourselves with the prayers of the psalmist and find that his God has not changed.


# 11 : Confession

## Psalm 51

In this the most penetrating of all the penitential psalms 'the uttermost depth of sin is grasped' (A. Weiser). The title relates the confession to David's acceptance of Nathan's rebuke after he had seduced Bathsheba and disposed of Uriah. It is an amplification of his acknowledgement: 'I have sinned against the Lord' (2 Sam. 12.13). There is no attempt to present a defence or to plead extenuating circumstances. Nor is there any appeal to previous righteousness as counterbalancing current guilt. The single-heartedness of David's confession reveals how completely his mind is dominated by the realization of his sin. The urgency and intensity of his pleas, coupled with the reiteration of the same expressions of contrition, indicate the depth and genuineness of his repentance.

He speaks of transgressions in the plural (1, 3), for his offences had multiplied. No sin ever stands alone. One invariably leads to another and even more. Nothing breeds so quickly as sin. Sin is here identified in terms of departure from the norm (transgression, vs. 1, 3), deflection from the ideal (sin, vs. 2, 3, 5), perversion of the right (iniquity, vs. 2, 5), and displeasing God (evil, v. 4). It is a debt to be cancelled or a record to be expunged (9), a stain to be removed with a detergent, and a disease to be cured by medication (7).

It is recognized as an inherited bias, but this is not allowed to degenerate into an excuse (5). The fact that the tendency to sin is innate does not relieve man of responsibility for the sins he willingly makes his own. Incidentally, we have here 'such a clear confession of original sin . . . . . that the spiritual affinity with Genesis 3 is incontestable,' according to Eichrodt. As he puts it, we have no need to go into 'exegetical wriggles' to evade this insight.

The psalmist realizes that although he has sinned grievously against others, his real offence is against God (4, cf. Gen. 39.9). The corollary of this recognition is that only God can relieve man of his guilt. Our society is sick because it fails to act on the implications of this truth.

# 12 : Moral Imperfection

## Proverbs 20.1–22

From ch. 16 onwards the writer of Proverbs assumes the existence of personal sins as distinct from national defection. The forms which such transgressions may take are varied. Amongst those catalogued here are intemperance (1), anger (2, cf. 19.12), contention (3), idleness (4, 13), fraud (10, 14, 17), gossip (19), disrespect for parents (20), greed (21), and revenge (22).

The possibility of an upright life is by no means ruled out. Indeed, it is set up as an ideal to be cherished (7). Nevertheless, while there are many who claim to be trustworthy, yet few pass the test (6). Profession is common; fulfilment is rare. So often offers of help prove hollow. It is not easy to find someone who can really be relied on in a time of crisis. Such is the fallibility of human nature that good intentions are seldom translated into corresponding acts. Man often means well but fails to do well. The final test is action (11).

Hence the admission of universal failure in v. 9, which

Eichrodt considers to have been accepted at this period as an axiom of belief. Who indeed can claim to have a completely clear conscience and to be purified from every stain of sin (cf. Job 15.14)? This declaration of man's moral imperfection was evidently the outcome of observation and reflection. The terms used here make it obvious that the reference is to moral and not to ceremonial uncleanness. Later Jewish teaching would claim that the attainment of moral perfection is the only means of getting right with God. In Ecclesiasticus 3.14f. a son's fulfilment of his duty towards his father in old age is said to be entered in the credit column of the ledger to counterbalance sins which because of this will melt like frost in the sun. No such scheme of salvation by works is in evidence here in Proverbs, nor, indeed, any hint that man is capable of producing righteousness at will.

*A thought: In the New Testament one word does service for the two ideas 'faith' and 'faithfulness'. If I am to be trustworthy my life must be grounded by faith on Him who is faithful.*

## 13 : The Emptiness of Life

### Ecclesiastes 1.1–18

The theme of Ecclesiastes is announced in v. 2. The author appears to state his conclusion at the outset as well as at the close (12.8). It is found no less than thirty-nine times altogether in the book. Here it is to be regarded as a proposition rather than a verdict. What follows in the successive chapters of Ecclesiastes is the evidence gathered largely from the Speaker's own experience. All human existence divorced from God is utterly frustrating and unsatisfying. Man out of touch with his Maker can never sort out the meaning of life or achieve integration and happiness.

It must be realized that the Speaker (*qôhelet*, the president of the assembly) is considering human experience from a purely this-worldly, materialistic standpoint. Omit the spiritual dimension and what does it look like? His perspective is 'under the sun' (14). This phrase recurs again and again (29 times) to remind us that the author writes within self-imposed

21

limitations. As, like space-age man, he searches for significance in 'all that is done under heaven' (13) he makes no reference to divine revelation. Can it be then that he is deliberately endeavouring to demonstrate man's total inability to solve the mystery of life apart from the light God gives? He is not an unqualified pessimist, as it might seem. His pessimism is confined to the prospects of disorientated man.

To man out of relation to God life presents itself as a wearisome cycle (3–11). There is a desolating sameness about it. It is rather like the headlines of the news today—the names and places change but what happens is sickeningly similar. Is life really getting anywhere? Because of this disenchantment man feels that all his energies are being wasted (3).

From v. 12 the Speaker begins to draw specifically from his own experience. He was noted as a seeker after wisdom. But at the end of all his investigations he decides that life is 'a sorry business' (13 NEB). He has only been chasing the wind (14, 17). More knowledge only brings more sorrow.

How modern all this seems! Novels, plays, films, poetry, painting, music—so much in all the art-forms of today combines to present us with one doleful message: everything is without meaning! And so it is—without Christ!


## 14 : Broken Cisterns

### Ecclesiastes 2.1–11

Like the rich man in Luke 12.18 f. the Speaker has a conversation with himself once more (cf. 1.16). He will try a further experiment. Instead of applying himself to philosophy, he will discover whether pleasure can bring him satisfaction. 'Enjoy yourself' is the motto of the worldly man. What does he get out of it? The answer is precisely nothing (1). He decides that laughter borders on madness, even controlled hedonism is futile, and the stimulus of alcohol is abortive (2 f.). How much more the uncontrolled hedonism of our permissive age!

Next he turns to culture in order to fulfil his creative instinct (4–6). There is a parallel to his experiment in Tennyson's *Palace of Art*, with the same unsatisfactory outcome. The quest for beauty and the aesthetic comforts of gracious living are incapable of meeting man's profoundest needs. The creature cannot be content with the creation. He requires the Creator too. Behind all forms he must find the reality.

In vs. 7–11 the Speaker relates how he acquired possessions in the hope that they might afford him satisfaction. The acquisitive instinct is inherent in man. The communist philosophy denies something that is basic to human life. The urge to possess is not in itself necessarily iniquitous; it may be no more than a collector's mania. But it can never bring ultimate fulfilment, and may easily get out of hand and degenerate into an obsession. The Speaker amassed wealth and with it all that wealth can provide. He owned land and property. His flocks and herds were larger than those of any of his predecessors (7b). He had a staff of household slaves to wait on him (7a). Singers of both sexes supplied music, whilst his harem was filled with concubines (if that indeed is the meaning of an uncertain Hebrew phrase in v. 8). No effort was spared to indulge his passion to possess. Yet when he adds it all up, it only amounts to emptiness and chasing the wind (11). No surplus swells his credit. What a rebuke to our materialistic age! The desire of the underprivileged for material things is understandable, but what shall we say of the mad pursuit of wealth and possessions by those who already have too much for happiness, but who are not 'rich toward God'? A man may gain the whole world and yet forfeit his life (Matt. 16.26).

## 15 : Wisdom and Work

### Ecclesiastes 2.12–26

The Speaker reports another stage in his search for happiness. Pleasure, culture and wealth have failed to satisfy him. Now he returns to his search for wisdom (12–17, cf. 1.17). It is noticeable that this had never been abandoned altogether. In his pursuit of pleasure and wealth, he allowed wisdom to be his guide (2.3, 9). Now he accords it priority.

He recognizes that it has its undoubted value, for light is preferable to darkness (13). He quotes what is evidently a proverb to the effect that the wise man sees ahead whereas the fool is content to grope in the dark (14). Even though this may be so, the same fate awaits all at the end (16, cf. Heb. 9.27). Death is the great leveller and both the wise and the foolish will be claimed by the grave. The same thought is found in Psa. 49.10 and Job 21.26. There is moreover no special remembrance of the wise, and as time passes everything will be lost in oblivion. These sombre if not cynical observations lead to an extreme revulsion from existence itself (cf. 2 Sam. 13.15; Isa. 1.14; Amos 5.21).

That is an attitude with which we are all too familiar today. Our society has sunk below the despair line, as Kierkegaard put it. There is a widespread disenchantment with life. It would seem that the only logical outcome is suicide and it is an escape route which is increasingly used. But most are deterred by the undefined fear of Hamlet's 'something after death'. They still cling to life even whilst they are pronouncing it hateful.

In vs. 18–23 the Speaker considers yet another area which might give him the satisfaction he seeks. Perhaps work will provide the answer. But he declares himself to be disillusioned about the merits of honest toil. Of what profit is it if after all his efforts he will have to leave his business to someone who has not deserved it and may not appreciate or develop it (18 f.)? The thought is enough to drive him to despair (20). So he concludes that only as God is seen in work and wisdom can they bring any satisfaction. There is no ultimate contentment apart from Him. 'He is the substitute for everything. Nothing can be a substitute for Him' (C. Bridges).

# 16 : The Folly of Folly

## Ecclesiastes 10.1–20

The section from 9.17 to 10.20 contains a collection of proverbial sayings about wise men and fools—a recurring theme in Ecclesiastes. Even a little folly spoils the effect of wisdom, just as dead flies turn the perfumer's ointment rancid. The analogy reminds us of Paul's allusion to the leaven in the dough (1 Cor. 5.6). The fool in Scripture is the man who disdains moral principles and lives as a practical

24

atheist. This kind of folly is far from dead. The particular word employed here in Ecclesiastes (*sakal*) implies an almost irrational obtuseness. Even a modicum of such an attitude can blight the whole character. It will determine not only the direction we face in life (2), but also our ultimate destiny (cf. Matt. **25**.31–46).

The Speaker proceeds to deplore the incidence of folly in high places (4–7). It can do untold harm. Its effect is to disturb the settled order of society. The revolutionary spirit displaces the natural rulers of men and reverses the normal roles (6 f.). It was the habit of tyrants to promote the base-born to positions of honour. To ride on horseback was usually the prerogative of the aristocracy. The Roman historian Justin explained that this was how freemen were distinguished from slaves amongst the Parthians. Cf. Esther **6**.8 f. But when the social order is overturned and it is the slaves who commandeer the horses whilst princes go on foot, anarchy threatens the welfare of the realm.

Verses 8–15 contrast the advantages of wisdom with the consequences of folly. Even in the practical matters of man's everyday occupation it is better to use discretion. Folly produces its own friction which increases the burden of work. In v. 16 the Speaker issues a warning against evil rulers. It is a tragedy for any country when a slave (NEB) has been thrust on the throne and his advisers begin the day with revelry instead of administering the affairs of state (cf. Isa. **5**.11).

Such teaching needs to be weighed carefully. Does it mean that the social order should be taken as fixed for all time? Was Wilberforce wrong in pressing for the emancipation of the slaves, and treating this as a matter of Christian concern? Is the writer's perspective a purely worldly one —given to us through inspiration as a warning of worldly vanity—which would have to be modified considerably in the light of other parts of Scripture and, perhaps, of the conclusion of his own book? It is well worth giving some thought to this matter.

Questions and themes for study and discussion on Studies 10-16

1. What does the Bible teach about the relationship between sin and disease?

2. How can man be held responsible for his sins if sin is an inborn tendency?

3. Is there any trace of the outlook of Ecclesiastes in the New Testament?

4. If modern secular man has succumbed to despair, how may the message of Christian hope be most effectively presented to him?

5. On the whole, contemporary man would feel more kinship with the writer of Ecclesiastes than did the European or American of the 19th century. Why?

# FOUR

## Fallen: The New Testament

### 17 : The Slavery of Sin

### John 8.30–47

The key to this passage is to be found in v. 32. Jesus there speaks about the emancipation which results from a knowledge of the truth. The Jews retort that as Abraham's descendants they have never experienced bondage. Clearly they have failed to grasp what Jesus meant.

In v. 34 He explains what kind of slavery He had in mind. In 'one of the most remarkable sayings ever uttered by our Lord' (W. Hendriksen) the announcement is made that universal sin implies universal slavery. All who commit sin are slaves to it and since all sin, all are slaves. Jesus does not spell out the details of this proposition, but its logic is not lost on His hearers. The proud distinction of Jews from Gentiles is obliterated, since basically all men are equal in the sight of God—equal in sin (cf. Rom. 6.16; 2 Pet. 2.19). Even the pagan philosophers agreed. Seneca declared that no bondage is more severe than that of the passions, and Plato wrote that liberty is the name of virtue and slavery the name of vice. Jesus then goes on to make a rather different application of the slave metaphor, indicating, however, that in every sense the truest freedom is to be found in Himself (35 f.).

A discussion then follows as to the ancestry of the Jews (39–47). Our Lord's refusal to recognize them as children of Abraham or of God may be applied to any who claim relationship to God by reason of national, family or ecclesiastical connections. Evidence of kinship is shown in resemblance.

The devil is described as a killer (cf. 1 John 3.15) and a liar (44). It was he who first introduced sin to man and death through sin (Rom. 5.12). It was by misrepresentation that he tempted Eve (Gen. 3.4), and he is still the one who deceives

27

the world (Rev. **12**.9). By nature every man is not only a slave of the devil but is his child and takes after his father. Only by grace can he become a child of God as he trusts in Christ who is the Truth (John **14**.6).

## 18 : Suffering and Sin

### John 9

Our Lord's encounter with a man afflicted by congenital blindness raised the issue of the relationship between suffering and sin. 'The question is as old as humanity' (J. H. Bernard). The first answer the disciples suggested was not a feasible solution. Since this man had been blind from birth only some far-fetched hypothesis of pre-existence could lend it support.

The second suggestion reflected the prevailing view in Judaism. The reply of Jesus, however, rejected both these theories. No doubt all suffering is in some way the result of sin, but that is only half the story, and this was not a case where a specific sin had incurred a specific penalty. A backward look traces the connection not indeed between sins and sins but between sin and sin, since all are born in sin (34). A forward look, however, discerns the providential purpose of God which utilizes such suffering to reveal His power.

Such questions are still asked. Blindness is not the only congenital condition which afflicts human beings. The disciples were puzzled but perhaps detached questioners. Such questions gain an added and often an anguished dimension when they are asked from within the family of the afflicted. Where mere human sympathy and wisdom are so inadequate, the words of Him who plumbed the depths of human sorrow and suffering at Calvary have a power to comfort which is all their own, as so many distressed yet trusting believers have discovered.

More serious than the physical blindness recorded here is the spiritual blindness of the Pharisees, because they are altogether unconscious of it (40 f.). Christ not only came that the blind might see, but also that those who claim to see might become blind (Mark **4**.12). The very fact that the Pharisees imagine they are equipped with spiritual vision aggravates their guilt. Archbishop Temple warned against trying to keep our eyes half open and to live by half the light. 'That kind of sight holds us to our sin and our sin to us.'

*A thought : What helps so much here is not only what is said but who it is that says it.*

## 19 : The Curse of Adam

### Romans 5.12–21

This is the most extensive New Testament commentary on the fall. The implications of Adam's sin are drawn out, and we are shown how the work of Christ as the last Adam reversed that of the first.

'All men sinned' (12) does not simply mean that at some time or other everyone has been guilty of transgression. The context makes it clear that what the apostle intends to affirm is the more fundamental fact that all sinned representatively when Adam sinned. Mankind is regarded as an organic unity. It is a single body under a single head. Adam is the head of the old aeon of death as Christ is the head of the new aeon of life. The sinful fate of humanity was representatively and historically determined in Adam in the same way that the road to salvation was opened up representatively and historically in Christ. In each case it was through 'one man' (12, 15–18), as representing all. The similarities and contrasts are worked out in a fivefold series (15–19).

'Death through sin' (12) is another recurring theme in this passage (14 f., 17, 21). The intrusion of death—and the reference here is to physical as well as to eternal death—is a consequence of the fall. Exile from Eden involved exclusion from the tree of life (Gen. 3.24). Paul tells us that death 'spread to all men' (12)—it made its way to each member of the human race and gained the mastery over them. All this was 'because all men sinned in Adam' (12). Recent translations support this traditional interpretation of *eph ho* as 'because' in preference to 'under these conditions' or 'in so far as'.

The relationship of sin to the law is considered in v. 13 and taken up again in vs. 20 f. Like sin and death, law too 'came in' (20). Its effect was to multiply sin. Sin, of course, was present in the world long before the law as such was introduced, but it could not be charged up. When the law was formulated, it intensified and in some instances even provoked transgression. The very prohibition sometimes adds an attraction to sin for the rebellious heart. Law, then, only aggravated the fall. But for 'grace abounding' man could never have recovered.

## Questions and themes for study and discussion on Studies 17-19

1. It has been said that man is only really free when nothing that can harm him has any power over him. Do you agree?

2. How can the biblical doctrine of providence be employed in seeking to help those perplexed by problems of human suffering and affliction?

3. Does Paul's teaching give us any idea as to *how* Adam's descendants become involved in his fall and its results?

# FIVE

## A Guilty Rebel: Recognized in the Old Testament

### 20 : Unconscious Offences

#### Leviticus 5

This chapter forms part of the Manual of Sacrifice (1.3–7.38) which from 4.1 to 6.7 gives instructions to the people about offerings for sin. 'We are dealing with sacrificial procedure having expiatory effects' (M.Noth). A special type of trespass is considered in 5.1–13, which is an appendix to ch. 4. It has to do with unconscious offences in which a man only realizes later that he has infringed the law. Even such lapses, however trivial they may seem, are regarded as sinful.

In the first case (1), someone fails to come forward and give evidence, even after there has been a public appeal. Of course, there may be a deliberate refusal to testify, but in the context a misunderstanding of the summons or a defective sense of duty is implied. The second is a case of cultic uncleanness through accidental contact either with an animal or a man (2 f.). The taboos are tabulated in chs. 12–15 and the penalty of excommunication prescribed (Num. 19.13, 20). If the purification has been omitted through ignorance, however, guilt can be covered by the sin offering. The third case is that of a rashly sworn vow (whether good or bad) which a man forgets he has made or does not realize is culpable (4). It is not clear whether the offering actually procures his release from the oath.

All these offences require confession of sin before the entire community (5 f.) and the presentation of the sin offering 'as his penalty for the sin that he has committed' (NEB). To translate as 'guilt offering' (AV, RV, RSV) is misleading since *asam* is here used non-technically (as also in v. 7).

Verses 14–19 deal with the guilt offering as such, although N.H. Snaith prefers to call it a compensation offering. The Jerusalem Bible has 'reparation'. The word has to do with

31

liability for repayment. Each of these cases involves fraud. 'The holy things of the Lord' (15) include the gifts and tithes which were the perquisites of the priests. If these were not up to standard, or actually withheld, and this was shown to be intentional, the death penalty could be imposed (Num. 15.31). But if it was an unwitting offence, restitution had to be made in full plus a twenty per cent fine. In the case of a completely unknown fault the compensation offering was required but not the compensation payment.

Man is regarded as responsible to God even when he sins in ignorance. Otherwise it would pay not to know. In fact, the passage teaches us that no transgression of the Law of God is to be viewed as of little account. Nothing which caused suffering to Christ (whose sacrifice is the antitype of all the Levitical offerings) can be treated as trivial by His redeemed.

## 21 : Not One Good

### Psalm 14

The psalm opens with a lament about the depravity of the wicked, cast, as Weiser explains, in the form of a prophet's forceful denunciation (1 ff.). The *nabal* is not merely a fool, but a much more aggressive character who is militant in his denial of God (1). Behind the devastating corruption that runs through the whole of society lies the refusal to recognize the existence of the moral claims of a holy God.

In a picture full of pathos, the Lord Himself is described as gazing down from heaven on all mankind to discover if any have enough sense to seek Him out. The conclusion of v. 3. is comprehensive. All without exception have proved disloyal ('turned aside' is used of going after other gods; cf. Exod. 32.8; Judg. 2.17). and are 'rotten to the core' (NEB). Not even one can be found who is not tainted by sin. It is this verse that Paul quotes in Rom. 3.10.

Even pagan writers have conceded the universal inclination of man to evil. Horace declared that no one is born without faults and that even if nature is driven away with a pitchfork it continually returns. The Jewish rabbis had to admit that even the most pious of the pious were nevertheless guilty in at least one direction. The trouble with modern man is that, although recognizing the same fact after a fashion, he tries to turn the edge of it by appeals to the 'animal nature' resulting from evolution or by some other natural factor. Sin is the last realm in which we want 'to call a spade a spade'.

The sins which spring from a rejection of God are indicated throughout the psalm. They include corruption (1), alienation (2), infidelity (3), cruelty (4), prayerlessness (4), and derision (6). These are only samples, for in fact 'every crime in the book' stems from the same source. That is why the Bible interprets sin as unbelief. It is more than breaking rules. It is a breach of fellowship between man and God. It is a fractured relationship. Those who in the spurious wisdom of their own conceit decide that there is no God cannot even begin to please Him. That is why atheism is the ultimate folly. It is a repudiation of God's sovereignty.

## 22 : The Lessons of History

### Psalm 78.1–31

Here we are invited to look into what Delitzsch called 'the warning mirror of history', in order to learn the lessons of the past. The psalmist conducts us through the archives of Israel from Moses to David. His purpose is not so much to focus our attention on antiquity as to show the relevance of previous events for our current situation. The philosopher Benedetto Croce has said that all history is contemporary in the sense that it has contributed to what is happening now and is thus part of the living present. This is especially true of redemption history.

In vs. 1–8 the psalmist indicates that he has a *maskil* (parable) to deliver (2). He will 'expound the riddle of things past' (NEB). Before he turns to God's miracle of deliverance at the Red Sea (12–13), he voices a complaint against the Ephraimites because of their defection (9 ff.). They are singled out from the rest of the tribes as being exceptionally reprehensible. They committed the unpardonable sin, militarily speaking: they deserted in the middle of a battle. An actual incident is not identified: it may have been a general reluctance to implement the conquest of Canaan.

We get some hints as to why they cracked under pressure. They shared the general deterioration of a spineless age. Their hearts were not fixed on God (8). There was a failure in orientation. Moreover, they proved unfaithful to the covenant which undergirded the whole relationship between Yahweh and His people (10a). They even set aside the demands of the law, refusing to walk along the path it laid down (10b). Worse still, they forgot what God had done (11). The recollection of His protecting mercy, which should have spurred them on to further exploits, had faded from their minds. This is how the devil still tempts us to quit the fight. We must be aware of his methods.

The overall failure of the Israelites themselves is pinpointed in v. 22. They did not fully trust in God nor did they really believe in His ability to rescue them (cf. Num. **14.**11). They did not realize that the exodus from Egypt was a sign of God's continuing help. They still dubiously enquired, 'Can God?' (19 f.). Doubt is a frequent ingredient of sin. Only when we are convinced that God can shall we gain the victory.


## 23 : A Portrait of the Heart

### Psalm 78.32–66

Persistence in sin (32), despite the marvels of God's intervening grace, deserves and receives His disciplinary chastisement (33). The reference may be to the judgement of death threatened on those of twenty years old and upwards after the departure from Egypt (Num. **14.**12, 28 ff.). The effect of this punitive measure was to jolt God's children out of their spiritual complacency (34). 'When he struck them, they began to seek him' (NEB).

But in vs. 36 f. we find that their repentance was unreal. They went through the appropriate motions and uttered the ritual incantations (36), but they still remained faithless at heart (37). They pretended to be contrite for fear of what might be visited upon them and not because they had a genuine love of righteousness. Yet even in the face of such dissembling, God restrained His wrath in compassion and

34

still continued to forgive (38). The long-suffering of God is movingly depicted.

The reason for His forbearance is disclosed in v. 39. It is that, as Psa. 103.14 expresses it, 'he knows our frame; he remembers that we are dust.' He took into consideration the moral helplessness of man. The reference to the flesh implies ethical impotence as well as the transitoriness of mortal life (cf. Gen. 6.3; 8.21). The repeated intransigence of the Israelites is contrasted with God's everlasting mercy in vs. 40–55. The section from v. 56 to v. 72 speaks of renewed rebellion, in particular through idolatrous entanglement (58). The sinful condition of God's people is graphically summarized in v. 57. They were like a bow with a warp (Jerusalem Bible) which cannot be used by the archer (Hos. 7.16). It lets the arrow fly off at a tangent. Even when the Israelites attempted to return to God, they deviated from Him and thus disappointed His expectations. No wonder their ingrained recalcitrance 'provoked most justly' His 'wrath and indignation'.

Such an historical psalm makes us aware of the fact that church history contains examples of similar sins, translated from national into ecclesiastical terms. And what of the individual? Do we not all have times of rebellion to confess? Is the Christian's penitence as deep as it should be? Where would *I* be without the long-suffering of God? And yet how unthinkable that I should ever presume on it in the face of Calvary!

## Questions and themes for study and discussion on Studies 20-23

1. To what extent do the Levitical regulations concerning unconscious offences bear on the Christian conception of sin?

2. Compare Psa. **14** with Psa. **53**. Can you suggest any *spiritual* reason why we should have been given two psalms that are almost identical?

3. Compare Psa. **78** with Acts **7**. What lesson do they teach in common? Do any other psalms deal with Israel's history as the story of her faithlessness and rebellion?

# SIX

## A Guilty Rebel: Convicted by the Prophets

### 24 : Sin Exposed

#### Isaiah 1.1–20

In what has been described as a prophetic fly-sheet the nation of Israel is indicted before God because of its apostasy. An appeal is made to witnesses amongst the angelic hosts above and to men on earth (2). Although the references are to the corporate sin of God's people, we cannot fail to be convicted personally by this trenchant denunciation. Sin is subjected to close analysis and is exposed in many aspects.

It is a revolt (2, 5, 20). This was the primal sin of man and rebellion is still of its essence. The word used here stands for the repudiation of authority. It can refer to rebellion against a ruler (1 Kings 12.19; 2 Kings 1.1), but in this case it has to do with a child's resistance to parental control. Sin is seen as stupidity (3). Even the less intelligent animals have the sense to know to whom they belong and where their welfare lies, but man is so foolish and ignorant that he refuses to recognize the only One who can help him.

Sin is a burden (4). The nation is loaded with guilt. Its back is broken and it is incapacitated. Sin is evildoing (4). It not only affects the sinner; it injures others. Sin is perversion (4). It involves a departure from God's way and leads to corruption and destructiveness (NEB, cf. Gen. 6.12). Sin is hereditary, for Israel is addressed as the offspring of evildoers (4, cf. Matt. 3.7). It is not enough to interpret this as meaning merely that the nation consists of evildoers. It does so by reason of descent.

Sin is desertion (4). The word translated forsaken means abandoned for another god (Judg. 2.11 ff.; 10.6, 10; Deut. 31.16). Sin is contempt (4). God's people have spurned Him. He is the Holy One of Israel but they reckon nothing of that. Sin is alienation (4). The children of God are now cut off from Him because they have turned from Him. Sin is a dis-

36

ease (5 f.). It has infected the body politic from head to foot.

In vs. 10–15 the prophet shows how impossible it is for those who cling to their sin to get right with God through the prescribed ritual. When divorced from righteousness, sacrifice amounts to no more than a bribe. The only hope of sinners lies in the pardoning love of God, if they will but return to Him. For us, too, religious observances and zeal for the church can blind us to our real need.


## 25 : Jerusalem Indicted

### Ezekiel 22

In three successive invectives Jerusalem is condemned for her sins and threatened with judgement. The first of these oracles (1–16) lists the crimes she has committed. The second (17–22) uses the analogy of the smelter's furnace. Israel has become an alloy—no longer pure silver—and the fire of God's anger will melt her people. In vs. 23–31 the fall of the city is foreshadowed and a roll-call of the guilty is drawn up, including all classes of society.

The sin of Israel reflects the sin of man in every age and place. We will often be reminded of our own fast-deteriorating society as we study this chapter. Sin manifests itself in violence and bloodshed (2 ff., 6, 9, 12 f., 27). Indeed, blood is the keyword of this passage. Jerusalem is a city of blood (3). Its last days before its collapse were marked by murders committed under the pretext of policy as well as the ritual slaughter of children (16.20 f., cf. 7.23; 9.9; 23.37, 39; 24.6, 9; 33.25; 36.18). Disrespect for parents led to a break-up in family life (7). The law required that children should honour both father and mother (Exod. 20.12; Lev. 19.3; Deut. 5.16), and to treat them with contempt was a capital crime (Lev. 20.9; Deut. 27.16).

Injustice was rife. Immigrants were amongst the victims. This is certainly not unknown today. Resident aliens were cheated by extortion (7, 29). Human rights protected by the Jewish law (Exod. 22.21; Lev. 17.8, 10, 13; 20.2) were callously ignored. Orphans and widows—the stock representatives of the deprived and underprivileged—were shamefully treated, again in contravention of the law (Exod. 22.22 ff.).

Informers procured bloodshed by slander (9), despite the prohibition of Lev. **19**.16, and received bribes (12), though this was denounced in Exod. **23**.8.

A sexually permissive society is berated in this comprehensive indictment and our own badly needs to hear these words. To 'commit lewdness' (9) is sometimes a figure for false worship, but in this context is to be taken literally. The expression occurs more often in Ezekiel's prophecy than anywhere else in the Old Testament. The law was explicit in its prohibition of adultery and incest (10 f., cf. Exod. **20**.14; Lev. **18**.7 ff., 15).

At the root of this galloping consumption of sin lay a forsaking of God for idols (3 f.). Here is the source of Jerusalem's defilement. Her people have despised the holy place (Jerusalem Bible) and profaned the holy day (8, 16, 26). They have even consumed idolatrous sacrifices at the mountain shrines declared illegal in the Deuteronomic reform (**6**.3; **16**.16; cf. Hos. **4**.13; Jer. **2**.20). Yet again Scripture insists that man without God is liable to be man without morals.

## 26 : National Sins

### Daniel 9.3–19

Daniel's prayer of confession is one of the most searching to be recorded anywhere in Scripture. It is reminiscent of other passages in its phraseology, although more than simply a mosaic of biblical quotations. It is addressed to God in His might and fearfulness (4a, cf. Deut. **7**.21). The sins of the nation are all the more heinous because they have been committed against One who keeps His covenant (4b).

A series of synonymous verbs in v. 5 indicates the multiplicity and variety of the people's sins. This is not empty repetition. These accumulated expressions suggest that sin is like the fabled hydra with many heads. Daniel acknowledges that 'all Israel' (7, 11) has been involved. God's children have failed to reach His standard, dealt perversely in wilful disobedience, done what is wicked out of inexcusable ingratitude, revolted from Him in irresponsible anarchy (9), and totally ignored His wise decrees. 'Commandments' are the contents of legislation, and 'ordinances' (lit. 'judgements') the legal decisions in particular cases which then became binding (5). Refusal to pay heed to God's servants the prophets—the spokesmen of His word—completes the catalogue of defection (6, 10).

The gist of the confession is contained in v. 7. Daniel freely admits that God is altogether in the right and he and his people are altogether in the wrong. There is no hint of self-justification. They have clearly lost face before God because of their treachery (a strong word, cf. Lev. 26.40; Ezek. 17.20). Even though they are aware of God's gracious compassion they nevertheless persist in rebellion (9).

By its infidelity Israel has brought down on itself the divine curse threatened long before (cf. Deut. 29.20; Num. 5.21). It is recognized that if God failed to reprimand sin He would be guilty of breaking His promises just as much as if He failed to protect the righteous. How often we purr when we receive God's favours but growl when chastised for sin.

Because of God's invariable faithfulness, Daniel dares to plead for restoration (15–19). It is not on the ground of their own righteousness (18), but only for the sake of God's honour (19). He calls on God to act in accordance with His revealed nature.

Along with Israel, 'Christian' nations have had great privileges and have abused them. The Christian cannot shut his eyes to the sins of his own nation, but neither can he stand over against it as if he had no part in its sins. Like Daniel, he will pray from within and will confess 'we have sinned, we have done wickedly'.

## 27 : Sin Next Door

### Amos 1

Amos 1.3–2.3 denounces the sins of Israel's neighbours. In 2.4–16 Judah and then Israel itself are accused. Greater light brings greater responsibility. These eight woes are all introduced by the same formula and follow the same overall pattern. 'Transgressions', as Snaith insists, should be translated as 'rebellious acts'. The Hebrew pešaʿ indicates revolt against God Himself rather than an offence against an individual. 'It is part of Amos's message that crime against anybody or anything whatsoever is crime against God' (E. A. Edgehill).

Amos makes no allusion here to ritual lapses. He is concerned with social and national righteousness. His prophecy is characterized by a burning ethical zeal. Men have displeased God by their cruelty, barbarism, contentiousness and belligerency. Sin is nothing short of a rebellion and can on no account be tolerated (Isa. 1.28).

The expression 'for three transgressions . . . . and for four' (3) suggests the indefinite multiplicity of these enormities. The rabbis taught that three transgressions might be forgiven but that four were beyond the limit. God will not now intervene to avert the inevitable retribution. His word of judgement is irrevocable (cf. Isa. 55.11). The repetition of these solemn warnings in each instance conveys an impression of unrelieved menace.

The order in which the nations are paraded before God to receive their sentence of doom is not that of place or time but of relation to Israel. The grim roll-call starts with Syria, the most oppressive of all Israel's enemies (3 ff.). It continues with the oldest—Philistia (6 ff.)—and then moves to Tyre, with whom Israel evidently had some sort of agreement (9 f.). Edom (11 f.) and Ammon (13 ff.) represented blood relations of Israel. Little does the latter realize, however, that the same inexorable judgement which the surrounding nations have incurred is overtaking them.

Modern history, especially that of Europe, furnishes some amazingly close parallels to some of the sins denounced here. It would be worth reviewing the history of the past few decades in search of parallels as a reminder that the Bible is astonishingly up-to-date and that human nature has not changed. Neither should one's own nation be ignored. We are always much more conscious of others' shortcomings than our own. God would bring us to face them, as He compelled Israel to face hers.

# 28 : Sin at Home

## Amos 2

Like the roll of approaching thunder the successive pronouncements of divine doom draw nearer and nearer to Israel. Moab is castigated for desecrating the body of an Edomite king (1 ff.)—perhaps a reference to 2 Kings 3.27. When judgement reaches Judah, Israel can no longer expect to escape (4 f.). Neglect of the law and idolatry are common to both. Perhaps we should recall that under the new covenant judgement is said to *begin* at the house of God.

A series of charges is listed in the actual indictment of Israel (6–16). Inhumanity, extortion and oppression are included, along with unchastity and apostasy. The instances cited in vs. 6, 7, however, do not involve the actual infringement of the law. But the money-mad business men of Israel craftily used it to serve their own acquisitive ends. We may keep on the right side of the civil code and yet sin against both God and man. Our attitude to *people* matters a great deal to God.

These oppressors would foreclose a mortgage so that the debtor had to be sold into slavery (cf. Lev. 25.29; Deut. 15.2). While for most of us slavery is a thing of the past, this kind of sin is not. The title-deeds of some poor man's inheritance would be seized and his land appropriated, if indeed v. 6b refers to the custom of selling land by the transfer of a shoe (Ruth 4.7; Psa. 60.8). The rich trampled down the very heads of the poor in the dust and pushed them aside as they hurried along the street. It is the underprivileged who invariably suffered, for, as E. B. Pusey pointed out, 'wolves destroy, not wolves, but sheep'.

The reference in v. 7b is not simply to sexual aberration but also to idolatry. In the debased religion of the period, sacred prostitution was part of the ritual pattern. It was a feature of the Canaanite cults as well as of the Babylonian temples. It could well happen that father and son resorted to the same girl. In these pagan shrines, pawned clothes were used to make rugs on which men prostrated themselves before the altar, and the wine they drank had been bought with money extorted from the poor (8). The Targum translates the plural *elohîm* here as 'idols', as if Amos were distinguishing them from the God of Israel. His name has been deliberately profaned (7b), but His judgement on sin is imminent (9–16). It is never wise to think of it as remote. 'Behold, the Judge is standing at the doors' (Jas. 5.9).

## 29 : The Unholy City

### Zephaniah 3.1–8

After announcing judgement on the nations in 2.4–15, Zephaniah returns in ch. 3 to arraign Jerusalem as he had already done in ch. 1 (cf. vs. 4, 10–13). He castigates afresh the sins that are rampant within all sections of the community, and most especially those in positions of responsibility (3 f.). Leaders are responsible not simply to man but to God, the Governor of all.

Rebellion is set at the head of the crime sheet (1). The people of Jerusalem have defied God and His standards. The verb means to resist insolently. There has been an obstinate refusal to pay any attention to the divine admonition and to submit to discipline (2). The city, moreover, is said to be polluted—no doubt by various sources of defilement, but in particular by bloodshed (Lam. 4.14; Isa. 59.3). Our own society is increasingly aware of the dangers of material pollution and increasingly careless of its moral counterpart. Jerusalem, reflecting an enduring characteristic of fallen man, is tyrannical in its oppression and exploitation of the under-privileged classes. The magistrates are so rapacious that they are compared with hungry wolves who devour all their prey as soon as it is killed and leave nothing over for the morning (or perhaps who had 'nothing to gnaw that morning' [Jerusalem Bible], and are thus more than ever voracious in the evening).

Even the religious leaders of Israel have fallen away from God. The prophets who ought to have been His spokesmen are unrestrained in their eagerness to gain cheap popularity (4). Beware the snare of preaching 'to the gallery'! As Jerome explained, 'they spoke as if from the mouth of the Lord and uttered everything against the Lord.' The priests profaned the sanctuary by their impiety and empty ritual and violated the law by twisting it to serve unworthy ends.

Even when God's punitive sanctions were applied men still

persisted in sin (4 f.). What had already befallen Jerusalem should have compelled the citizens to take stock of their condition and return to the Lord. Instead, they only grew more refractory, even rising early to go about their wicked ways. It is because of this deliberate and aggravated disobedience that final judgement will fall.

The root of Jerusalem's sin is disclosed in v. 2b. It sprang from a failure in trust. The prophets unanimously insisted on faith as a *sine qua non* (Isa. 7.9; Jer. 17.7). If we trust God we can no longer place our reliance on self or others.

**Questions and themes for study and discussion on Studies 24-29**

1. Isa. 1.1–20 exposes sin in a number of aspects. Complete the list from other biblical references.

2. 'When God is not, everything is changed and everything is allowed' (Sartre). Consider this in the light of the biblical revelation.

3. What other great biblical prayers reveal the intercessor's sense of involvement in the sin of those for whom he prays?

4. Social injustice figured prominently in Amos's indictment of Israel's sin. How far do Christians fail to recognize this factor today?

5. What are the abiding sins of city-life?

# SEVEN

## A Guilty Rebel: Recognised and Rebuked in the New Testament

### 30 : The Need to Repent

### Luke 13.1–9

It has to be recognized that, as Earle Ellis points out, 'in the Gospels Jesus does not speak to the question of original sin'. He never discusses it. He simply assumes the universality of sin and regards death as its consequence.

In Luke 13.1–9 an appeal for repentance continues the trend of the previous chapter with its warnings against hypocrisy and contention. Two instances are cited where fatalities had occurred. Although the connection between sin and death is maintained, it is not presumed that the victims were necessarily being punished for any particular offence or that their sin was more heinous than that of others. Indeed, the thrust of our Lord's comment is just the reverse. Unless all repent they too will 'come to the same end' (vs. 3, 5 NEB). If we are spiritually sensitive we should learn lessons likewise from the news items of our day.

Jesus repudiated any doctrinaire theory of retribution. The emphatic negative (3, 5) dismisses Jewish assumptions of this sort. Those who lost their lives in Pilate's massacre (1ff.) or in the accident at the tower of Siloam (4 f.) were not exceptionally wicked. They were ordinary men. Our Lord's purpose is to call His hearers to repentance. He invites them to consider their own sins and their own destiny, rather than to speculate about original sin. Understanding may sometimes need to wait but repentance should never be left until later.

The story of the fig tree in vs. 6–9 urges the need for a speedy response to the grace of God since the time is short. The fact that God is merciful with the sinner must not lead him to take advantage of the divine goodness. God will not wait for ever. The age of grace will eventually close. The expressions 'three years' and 'next year' should not be pressed literally in an application to our Lord's ministry. They simply denote the extension of God's grace (2 Pet. 3.15a). But there is an 'if not' (9). Unless the interval is used for repentance, judgement must fall. 'Therefore never send to know for whom the bell tolls: it tolls for thee' (John Donne).

# 31 : The Tyranny of Sin

## Romans 1.18–32

Paul's exposé of human sin and depravity finds its echo today in almost every news bulletin. He begins by describing the original status of man as a being to whom the knowledge of God was revealed. Since then, despite the fall, man has been unable to plead ignorance as an excuse (20, 32). The apostle is not subscribing to some deistic natural theology, but recognizing the extent of general revelation.

Sin is here seen as self-determination. It is the promotion of one's own opinions and desires to constitute the norm of conduct instead of seeking the divine will (21). So far from acquiring wisdom by these self-centred speculations, man shows himself to be basically stupid (22). He tends to look down on Christians as naïve and foolish in their belief, but in fact it is he who is so in his unbelief.

Sin is seen as idolatry. Whatever a man cannot live without is his god. The keyword is 'exchange' (23, 25). Something else has been put in the place of God. As a result, man prefers shame to His glory and a lie to His truth. The seat of sin is not to be located in the body but in the self. In the devastating catalogue of enormities from v. 26 onwards the sins of the mind and the soul are included as well as those of the body, as in Gal. 5.19 ff. Verses 24–27 list sins against nature and vs. 28–32 sins against society. It is an oversimplification to equate sin solely with the animal appetites. It may even be a device for evading the Divine condemnation on the sins He hates most—such as spiritual pride.

The result of sin is more sin. That is its immediate penalty. Man becomes an addict. Sin is against God, so God is against sin (18). He abandons man to its effects. Three times over we

45

are told that 'God gave them up' (24, 26, 28). He removes His restraining hand from man and lets licence lead to its own drastic consequences. 'When man does not turn to God, God punishes him by giving him up to sin' (A. Nygren),

## 32 : Secular Morality

### Romans 2.1–16

So far in his indictment of the moral collapse in the Roman Empire Paul would have carried many of his readers with him. As the apostle implies in Phil. 4.8 f., there were pagans who practised virtues which a Christian must emulate and indeed surpass. They would be as disgusted as we are at the grosser sins of society, but they would claim that they themselves were not implicated. This is the attitude the Jews would take too. Paul deals with them in 2.17–3.20, but in 2.1–16 he is probably tackling the secular moralists who have their counterparts today,

As K. J. Foreman points out, Paul does not explain his argument nor indeed substantiate it up to the hilt. 'He just tosses out the hand grenade and lets the splinters hit where they will.' Those who regard themselves as ethically superior and who would quickly condemn the moral landslide of the times are in fact guilty of sin themselves (1). Their vulnerability is exposed in a series of questions in vs. 3, 4. Despite their lofty ideals, they are still liable to lapse. They are only storing up the worst sort of trouble for themselves at the end of the age—the wrath of God which cannot condone sin. If God is at present gracious towards them, it is that they may be led to repent. That is the absolute condition of man's reconciliation with his Maker.

Verses 6–11 lay stress on the certainty of final retribution. It is performance that will count at the day of judgement (Psa. 62.12b). This is not a retrogression to salvation by works. Paul is simply demonstrating the inability of the moralist as such to achieve the righteousness God requires. Apart from the reception of grace in Christ, man is inherently incapable of satisfying God's moral demands, no matter how noble his aspirations may be. Those who choose to be assessed solely on deeds will be condemned by that criterion, for God has no favourites (11).

It is made plain in vs. 12–16 that Gentiles will not be penalized for their failure to observe a code inaccessible to them, but will be judged according to the light they have. Paul does not say that they possess the law, but that its demands are inscribed on their hearts, and their consciences tell them whether they have met its requirements or not.

*A question: Even if I feel relatively secure in reading ch. 1, what is my reaction to ch. 2?*

## 33 : The Depth of Inbred Sin

**Romans 3.1–20**

After dealing with a series of casuistical objections raised by Jews in vs. 1–8, Paul proceeds to show that all men without exception are not only subject to the dominance of sin (9) but in fact have actually committed sin (10–18). 'Psycho-analysis confirms what the pious were wont to say', wrote Sigmund Freud, 'that we are all miserable sinners'. In this respect Jews are in no better case than Gentiles, Paul argues.

On scanning the catena of Old Testament passages strung together after a familiar rabbinical fashion, the reader might be tempted to conclude that the verdict is too severe. Not everyone is like that. Paul is not suggesting that they are. 'Total depravity' does not demand that every possible kind of sin should necessarily assemble in each personality. It does imply, however, that all these symptoms of corruption are found in humanity as a whole. In a fallen temple not every block of stone may be broken or defaced in the same way, but each is nevertheless part of the ruin.

As Karl Barth insisted, the doctrine of original sin is not merely one amongst many, but, according to its fundamental meaning, the doctrine which emerges from an honest consideration of history. Men are unaware of what alone can redeem life from its inherent tragedy and bring them true integration and fulfilment. They are blind to the only way that will lead them to peace because they lack any reverence for God (17 f.).

The moral law is universal. It includes all in its condemnation. Every excuse is silenced and mankind is held answerable to God (19). The effect of law is to awaken a realization of sin. But it is incapable of removing it. Hence no man can get right with God along that line. A new method must be found. What it is Paul discloses in the next section (21–26).

## 34 : Disobedience and Disloyalty

### Hebrews 3

Heb. 3.1–4.13 is occupied with God's call to man to enter into His rest. After a reminder in vs. 1–6a that Christ was faithful as a son like Moses as a servant (5), the author stresses the urgency of the call and the response it requires (6b–15). Verses 7–11 contain a quotation from Psa. **95**.7–11.

A warning is issued against spiritual obduracy (8). Scripture elsewhere teaches that it is God who hardens men's hearts (Exod. **7**.3; Isa. **63**.17; Rom. **9**.18), and in v. 13 the verb is passive. But it is what Calvin described as 'spontaneous obstinacy', since man contributes to it by assuming that he can trifle with grace. He puts God to the test by venturing as far as he dares into sin without apparent danger. As a result, he becomes like a planet that has wandered from its orbit (10).

The source of such persistent disobedience lies in 'that wickedness of heart which refuses to trust' (Phillips). Disloyalty is implied as well as unwillingness to believe. Some commentators see here at least a verbal resemblance to the evil inclination (*yeser hara'*) of rabbinical literature. The result of such inner distrust is apostasy. Grotius distinguished between two kinds of unbelief: rejection of the truth when it is first presented and, more seriously, after it has been professed. It is this latter which the writer of Hebrews has in mind (cf. **6**.1–8). Hence the 'if' in vs. 6 and 14.

The failure of Israel to respond to the divine call is unambiguously attributed to the sin of unbelief (19). *Apistia* (unbelief, 12, 19) is contrasted with *pistos* (faithful, 2, 5). The lesson would not be lost on the readers of Hebrews. They too had experienced God's grace: they too might fail to enter into the promised rest through disobedience (18) and infidelity (19).

The regular use of Psa. 95 in worship in the Anglican communion is salutary. It is good for the Christian to be reminded that the blessings of the New Covenant, like those of the Old, are accessible only to faith, and that he should never become complacent about sin.


## 35: Sin as Lawlessness
### 1 John 3.4–18

The definition of sin in v. 4 is reversible. Lawlessness is sin and sin is lawlessness. *Anomia* (lawlessness) is in itself a negative concept which indicates a lack of conformity to the revealed will of God. But in Scripture it acquires a positive flavour and denotes active opposition to the law. 'To commit sin is to break the law' (NEB). See Matt. 7.23; literally 'you who do lawlessness'.

Lawlessness is not, of course, an all-inclusive description of sin. But it serves to reduce it to its basic element. Sin is doing wrong. That stark fact needs to be spelled out unambiguously. This is what makes sin the precise opposite of righteousness. 'The one doing the lawlessness' (4) is contrasted with 'the one doing the righteousness' (7). See v. 10 and 2.29.

John's readers are fully aware that Christ came into the world in order to remove sins—not merely to bear them but to bear them away. The effect of His atoning death is nullified if we persist in sin (cf. Rom. 6.1 f.). He is the sinless One who was sent to undo the devil's work (8). Hence the Christian does not make a habit of sin (note the present tense in vs. 6, 9). He may on occasion fall into a single act of sin (2.1 aorist), but he never makes a practice of it.

The 'seed' (AV) in v. 9 has been variously interpreted. Moffatt took it to mean children and translated 'the offspring of God remain in him' (i.e. in God). C. H. Dodd and others prefer to see in it the principle of divine life which resides in the regenerate—hence 'God's nature' (RSV). By reference to 1 Pet. 1.23–25 the seed is linked with the Word of God. But elsewhere in Scripture we find that it is the Holy Spirit who imparts and maintains new life. John confirms this in

49

v. 24 (cf. **2**.20, 27). We may perhaps adopt Greville Lewis's paraphrase, 'a principle of new life, imparted by God through the Holy Spirit, abides in the man who is born of God.' Hence sin is dealt with not by repression but by displacement.

Sin which is natural in the unbeliever is unnatural in the child of God. To transgress is to go against his renewed nature: 'he cannot sin' whilst he is true to what God has now made him. Sin is a contradiction of sonship (10).

## Questions and themes for study and discussion on Studies 30-35

1. Compile a series of passages from the Gospels illustrating our Lord's call to men to repent.

2. 'The sin of man'; 'the wrath of God against the sin of man'—which is the more appropriate summary of the teaching of Rom. **1**.18–3.20?

3. Why should Paul begin the main theological part of 'Romans' in the way he does? What would have been lacking if he had proceeded straight from **1**.17 to 3.21?

4. Might Heb. **3** and **4** suggest to our minds that restlessness is an element in, or a result of, sin? If so, which?

5. 'Self-coronation, including subtle, unconscious self-coronation—that is the essence of sin' (Vincent Taylor). What passages of Scripture bear out this statement?

6. Consider the relevance of Phil. **4**.8 f. to the question of secular morality. The verb translated 'think about' can also mean 'take into account'.

# EIGHT

## A Helpless Slave

### 36 : Inner Uncleanliness

### Matthew 15.1–20

The rite of purification was regarded by the legalistic Jewish leaders as a test case to distinguish between piety and laxity. They suspected that Jesus was not sound on this matter. A deputation arrives from Jerusalem to question Him about His disciples' behaviour. Our Lord does not give a direct answer. Instead He challenges the whole system of externalism.

He exposes the hypocrisy of His critics by showing that in fact they themselves only pay lip-service to the law when it suits their book (5 f.). They are ready to contravene the fifth commandment for the sake of a rash vow (itself regarded as incurring guilt in Lev. 5.4). This is nothing short of idolatry, for it allows traditional authority to usurp God's rightful place.

Then in vs. 10–20 Jesus deals with the underlying question of defilement. He insists that it is not primarily ceremonial but moral. It is the inward disposition not the external appearance which disqualifies a man from fellowship with God. Uncleanness comes from within and not from contacts without. It is not what goes into the mouth which defiles, but what comes out of it.

Jesus had spoken in a guarded way, although the lesson He intended to convey was plain enough. The disciples, however, demand a fuller explanation and in vs. 17–20 our Lord spells out unambiguously what He meant. Without actually speaking of sin He shows how it finds expression in the offences listed in v. 19 which infringe the commandments from Six to Nine. Evil thoughts lead to murder (6th.), adultery, fornication (7th.), theft (8th.), perjury and slander (9th.). This is the real source of uncleanness. Merely to omit the ablutions prescribed by tradition (not by the law itself) does not necessarily imply a sinful condition (cf. Luke 11.37–41). The most serious defilement is moral rather than ceremonial. Jesus could hardly have more forcibly stressed the inwardness of sin and the need to cleanse the central springs of human personality (Prov. 4.23; Jer. 17.9).

*Questions: What elements of externalism exist in contemporary religious life which tend to hinder the recognition of man's inner uncleanness? How can the situation be remedied?*

## 37 : The Way of Salvation
### 1 Corinthians 1.18–31

Paul is dealing with God's method of salvation. He contrasts the false wisdom with the true. The message of the cross reaches two classes of men: those who are on the way to destruction and those who are on the way to salvation (18). There is a clear-cut distinction here. It is the consistent insistence of Scripture that all of us must be either saved or lost. There is no third category, no half-way house between heaven and hell. As Jesus Himself taught, the broad way leads nowhere but to destruction (Matt. 7.13). To take it is the height of folly.

From v. 20 to v. 25 the apostle shows that even human wisdom (let alone human folly) is incapable in itself of conveying the knowledge of God. Corinth, like all Greek cities, would have its share of philosophers and other intellectuals. Our slavery of sin touches every part of our nature. Our minds are affected by sin, because any thinking which does not begin from God (not simply the general conception of deity, but the recognition of the true and living God) is bound to go astray in some way. 'Earth-bound' thinking is thinking in bondage. Types of thinking may change and the Platonism and Stoicism of the Greeks may be out of fashion today, but modern existentialism with its stress on the individual's quest for self-fulfilment falls just as much under the judgement of the cross.

The truth is that God has designed only one way of salva-

52

tion, and no other. The cross was not brought in as an after-thought. It was the ordained means of redemption from the beginning. An offence to sign-seeking Jews and nonsense to philosophical Greeks, Christ crucified is in fact both the power and the wisdom of God (22 ff.). God's apparent foolishness and weakness are superior to human wisdom and strength (25).

In the final paragraph Paul provides a window on the church in Corinth. Here is a breakdown of its composition in terms which would nowadays fascinate any sociologist. Not many intellectuals, not many of the influential, not many aristocrats, are to be found in the congregation. According to the world's standards it is an assembly of nonentities. But God can use the lowest of the low, and even 'those who are nothing at all, to show up those who are everything' (Jerusalem Bible).

## 38 : Freedom from Sin

### Romans 6.1–14

The questions in v. 1 were suggested by the closing paragraph of the previous chapter (5.18–21). The one trespass of Adam multiplied into the many trespasses of his descendants. Are we therefore to infer from this that our sins are to be increased in order that we may gain further opportunities for God's superabundant grace to be displayed? Paul's own initial hostility to the gospel had been met with overflowing grace (1 Tim. 1.13). Should we then deliberately plunge into sin in order to achieve a similar result?

Such antinomian policies are altogether inconceivable. We are not to do evil so that good may come (3.8). The Christian no longer lives in sin. He must not take advantage of God's grace. 'God will forgive me. It is His trade,' said Heine on his deathbed. But, as Foreman reminds us, God is not a vast forgiving machine. Justification is not the last word of evangelical doctrine. In its biblical content it is inseparable from sanctification. The Christian's baptism symbolizes his death to sin so that he might be raised to new life in Christ (4).

'With him' is the clue to the section from vs. 5–11. The old self was nailed to the cross with Christ. The body, of which sin had formerly taken possession, is no longer enslaved by sin. So far as sin's approach is concerned, it has been put out of commission. It is no longer at sin's disposal. This liberation from sin's bondage is achieved by death. When a man dies he is released. But Paul here transcends any courtroom concepts. He has moved to an entirely new dimension. This freedom from sin is made possible by the death of Christ. In Him a victory has been gained 'that needs no second fight and leaves no second foe'.

In 5.17 death reigned because of Adam's transgression. Here Paul pleads that sin may no longer reign, since Christ has died (12–14). It would be futile to urge sinners not to let this tyrant oppress them unless the news could first be conveyed that he has already been overcome. It is in our mortal bodies that sin still attempts to gain control. This mortality was brought about by original sin and will remain. The possibility of conquest is offered even within the limitations of the flesh. Sin need not lord it over us. In the sphere of grace, it can be subdued.

## 39 : Release from Slavery

### Romans 6.15–23

The question raised in v. 1 is repeated and reconsidered. Paul employs an analogy from slavery in order to illustrate the Christian's release from the domination of sin. If we are to appreciate its force we need to understand something of the place of slavery in the Roman empire. When a master bought a slave, he took him over completely. There was nothing the slave could call his own. He was in complete subjection. Such is the condition of the natural man with respect to sin.

Paul points out that this is how we once were (17, 20). We persistently presented ourselves as the serfs of sin (16, 19). It was a willing obedience. But all we got out of it was spiritual death. 'Fruit' is only used by Paul in a good sense (Gal. 5.22; Eph. 5.9; Phil. 1.11). It is the works of darkness which are unfruitful (Eph. 5.11). No worthwhile harvest can be gathered from the service of sin.

The Christian, on the other hand, is emancipated from this

slavery (18, 22). This is the release from bondage which restores man to the status he lost in the fall. Sin has usurped the authority which really belongs only to God (5.12 f.). We were never meant to be in chains. God created us for freedom in dependence on Himself. We might expect Paul to contrast the bondage of sin with the liberty of the righteous. Instead, paradoxically, he speaks about the new delightful submission involved in being a slave of Christ (18 cf. 1.1). To regard this simply as an unfortunate paradox is to overlook the biblical insistence that man's truest freedom springs from his obedience to God.

For the Christian there is a genuine harvest. The return he gets is sanctification (22). It leads to life everlasting—the opposite of death in v. 21. Both begin now and determine the future. Verse 23 offers a threefold contrast between wages and gift, death and life, sin and God. Sin is a master who pays his slaves with death. This is the grim recompense incurred by Adam's first disobedience, but not paid out until the end. 'The servant of sin gets the only wages sin can pay' (G. R. Cragg). The free gift of God in pure grace is eternal life. Whereas the result of sin passed automatically to all men, the gift of God procured by the death of Christ becomes ours only through faith.

# 40 : Anatomy of Sin

## Romans 7.7–25

In this piece of autobiography Paul analyses his own experience of sin and his struggle to master it. Some commentators take vs. 7–13 as referring to his condition before conversion, and vs. 14–25 as reflecting his conflict even as a Christian, although perhaps only a carnal one (14). But others contend that there is still much to be said for the interpretation of the early Church which related the whole passage to Paul's pre-conversion reaction to the law. Verses 7–13 then allude to his state before he was confronted by the challenge of God's moral demand, whereas vs. 14–25 describe his tragic dilemma as an earnest Pharisee, knowing full well what he ought to do yet finding himself quite incapable of achieving it.

The first paragraph deals with the dawn of conscience. The link between the law and the origin of sin is recognized as in 1 Cor. **15**.56. It is the law which makes man aware of the distinction between good and evil, and thus sets the stage for the contest which Paul describes (7, cf. 3.20). It is noticeable that the apostle focuses attention on the tenth commandment with its prohibition of covetousness. This is the one requirement of the Decalogue which penetrates beneath the surface of man's conduct and examines his inner motivation. Jesus was to do the same with respect to other commandments (Matt. **5**.21 f., 27 f.).

Law also stimulates the desire to sin (8 f., 11, 13). It provides sin with a base of operations. So sin springs to life again and resumes its murderous work. The false security of the ignorant sinner is disturbed by the law. He realizes that he is facing a killer (11). Sin is out to slay, and the effect of the law is to make him aware of its lethal intentions. It reveals the deadly nature of sin and the sheer inability of even the most morally determined of men to break loose from its fatal grip. The fault, as Saul the Pharisee had discovered, lay not in the law as such, which was all that it should be in itself (12), but in his own sin-bound nature (14). Hence the frustration expressed so agonizingly in vs. 15–20.

K. E. Kirk described vs. 17–20 as 'a parenthesis on the lower self'. Paul is dealing not only with flesh but actually with sin (17, 20). Verse 24 is a cry from the heart echoed by all who are prepared to face the truth about themselves. The deliverance for which Paul longs is not from his body as such, but from that which subjects his body to death through the power at work in his members, namely, the principle of sin within. A present though not final emancipation is assured in Christ (24 f.) and made possible by the Spirit (8.2 ff.). On this interpretation v. 25b simply summarizes the state of things before this intervention.

*A thought : The most noticeable word in this passage is 'I'. What can I learn from that?*

# 41 : Man's Natural Condition

## Ephesians 2.1–10; 4.17–19

In the Greek 2.1–10 forms one long sentence. It deals with the remarkable quickening which takes place in the life of one who is delivered from the slavery of sin and shares the victory of Christ. The opening verses describe the plight of such a man before the work of the Spirit begins. This is how the Ephesians and we ourselves once were—spiritually dead and alienated from God (1). Our condition was brought about by our rebellious acts and our sins. The two terms ('trespasses and sins') are used in combination to stress the gravity of this cause of our spiritual death, and the plurals indicate the continuity of its effect.

This was the sphere we formerly occupied. We took the way of the world and lived in terms of this present evil age. We were under the control of Satan, who is represented as the unholy spirit (2). As Christians are filled with the Holy Spirit and directed by Him, so those who rebel against God are activated by the evil spirit. Our old life was dominated by the desires arising out of our fallen nature. As Paul declares in Rom. 7.18, nothing good dwells in the flesh. Here then is our natural state—we are subject to God's wrath and fury (Rom. 1.18; 2.5, 8).

Wrath and fury are the unvarying reactions of God's holiness and righteousness against sin. He cannot condone it if He is to be true to Himself. 'By nature' (3) refers to inbred sin. Although the word (*physis*) may sometimes imply that which is habitual (and so 'second nature', as we say), it is regularly used to indicate what is innate. This is human nature at its conception and birth (Psa. 51.5). Paul is alluding to what is commonly known as original sin—man's congenital depravity as taught throughout Scripture. What is born of the flesh is flesh and thus tainted from the start (John 3.6). Verses 4–10 proceed to speak of the quickening the Spirit brings.

In the other passage (4.17–19) we have a further reference to the conduct of unbelievers. The Ephesians are urged to avoid the behaviour of the Gentiles who are cut off from God because of their inability to comprehend spiritual truth (18). This is not the ignorance of those who have failed to accept knowledge: it is an inborn ignorance which results from original sin. Hence their intellect is blinded and the heart grows callous to spiritual influences. This blunting of the moral sense leads to permissive behaviour of every kind. Futility (17) marks all that we did as unregenerate. The word means that which fails to lead to the goal. Unbelievers are off course in life. They will never find happiness and integration. They are engaged in a wild goose chase which gets them nowhere. What a contrast to the fulfilled life of the Christian!

## 42 : Strife Within and Without

### James 4.1–10

There is a startling transition from 'peace' (3.18) to 'wars' (4.1). What follows sounds like an account of our belligerent and acquisitive society today. But man has always been like this. Sin expresses itself in much the same way in every generation.

The reference in v. 1 is to private quarrels rather than to international wars. There is strife between man and man because there is strife within each man. We are ourselves by nature a walking battle-ground, and this inner conflict is perpetuated and indeed aggravated in our social relationships. If we cannot live at peace with ourselves, we are hardly likely to live at peace with others (cf. Rom. 7.23; 1 Pet. 2.11).

Man continuously craves for what he does not possess. There is a persistent voice within him which cries, 'I want,' When life replies, 'You can't,' he stamps his foot and shouts, 'I must, I will.' Here is what underlies our unrest today. The endless procession of desire, frustration and violence within unredeemed human nature has already been mentioned in 1.13–15.

Verses 4 f. constitute a sharp aside. James turns on his readers and accuses them of being as faithless as adulterous wives. Sin is represented in terms of marital infidelity. To make the world our friend is to make God our enemy. It is impossible to serve God and mammon (Matt. 6.24). Love both for the world and God are incompatible with each other (1 John 2.15).

Verse 5 is a puzzling one. No actual Scripture says what is recorded here, although several passages are in line with it (Gen. 6.5; 8.21; Prov. 21.10). Calvin bemoaned the fact that the text had worried many interpreters and had been worried by them! Perhaps it is preferable to punctuate the verse somewhat differently and thus obviate the question of direct quotation altogether. 'Do you think the Scripture is meaningless when it speaks on this subject (i.e. worldliness)? No: God yearns jealously over the spirit He has set within us.' If this is indeed the correct interpretation, then we realize how solicitously God watches over every man.

Despite man's rebellion, God continues to pour out the abundance of His grace. It is those who are prepared to give in to God who will be enabled to withstand the evil one (7).


## 43 : Advice for Transgressors

### James 4.11–5.6

The apostle's mood suddenly changes at 4.11 from denunciation of sin to reasoning with the sinner. He pleads with his readers to realize what they are doing when they indulge in malicious criticisms of one another, and his words are applicable to us also. When we do this we are in fact presuming to set ourselves above the law and in so doing we bring it into disrepute.

James probably has in mind the royal law of love (2.8) which, as interpreted by Jesus, goes beyond the bare demands of Mosaic legalism. Any attempt to denigrate a brother in Christ represents an affront to the supreme ideal of love. To judge another is more than merely foolish. It amounts to spiritual arrogance of the worst sort. We usurp the divine prerogative when we pass judgement on others. The stern warning of Matt. 7.1 must have haunted James' memory, for how could he ever forgive himself for the way in which he had judged Jesus (cf. John 7.3 ff.)?

In v. 13 the apostle confronts a different group. He rebukes those who fail to recognize that all life is under the providence of God. He addresses the business men of his time who have succumbed to the canker of materialism. The spiritual dimension has disappeared from their calculations. In their preoccupation with their business activities they proceed to arrange their schedules as if there was no God to reckon with. James might have been writing about today's commercial rat race! 'Great God, whither is man fallen?' wrote Thomas Mann. 'First we practise sin, then defend it, then boast of it. Sin is first our burden, then our custom, then our delight, then our excellency!'

In v. 17 James enunciates a general principle. If I know what is right and yet fail to do it, then for me that omission is sinful. No amount of casuistry can relieve me of responsibility. Yet even if we would heartily repudiate the approach of Jesuits and other experts in casuistry we may be guilty of choosing our path of conduct on expediency rather than on divinely-given principle.

Chapter 5 opens with an indictment of irresponsible plutocrats who live in style and devote themselves to the pursuit of pleasure whilst oppressing the innocent, helpless poor. The 'Rachmannite' may imagine that he is getting away with it. But he is only storing up retribution for himself (3). Judgement is inevitable and all such injustice—whether ancient or contemporary—cries to high heaven, as we would say (4). Sin still brings its own awful condemnation.

## 44 : False Doctrine

### 2 Peter 2

The second major section of Peter's letter contains his warning against the danger of false teachers and a vehement denunciation of their tactics. He begins by recognizing the fact of their existence and indeed of their inevitability. Jesus Himself had spoken about wolves who would consume the flock (Matt. 7.15–23). As there have been false prophets in the past pretending to have received direct revelations from heaven, so they will be paralleled in the Church by false teachers who distort the truth of the gospel. They will insidiously introduce their own speculations. 'Heresy' stands for self-willed choice, an error which a man insists on asserting in opposition to the apostolic doctrine. In many ways, Peter might have been writing of the twentieth century. We face today an almost unprecedented number of sects, each with its own peculiar doctrines. Some profess a 'higher' truth than that of Scripture, others interpret the Bible in a way that is literally eccentric, i.e. 'off-centre', for the Centre of Scripture is Christ. Such deceivers bring swift destruction on themselves and on those who fall for their perversion of the gospel (1). So serious is any deviation from the truth that it is tantamount to the repudiation of Christ Himself. The Christian way is brought into disrepute (2).

In vs. 4–10 Peter enlarges on the condemnation that awaits such misleading instructions. He picks out three outstanding examples from the past to back up his argument (cf. Gen. 6.1–4; 6.5 ff.; 19.24 f.). These instances are cited (4–6) to show how God does not allow the wicked to escape punishment, but holds them in Hades until the day of judgement (9).

The two sides specially underlined in v. 10a are sexual laxity and disregard for authority, which are in fact the two most obvious expressions of man's sin at the present time. From v. 10b to the end of ch. 2 Peter elaborates on the evil characteristics of the false teachers (cf. Jude 8–13). Irreverence lies at the root of their deviations, for they do not even shrink from reviling 'the glorious ones' (celestial creatures), or the glories of Christ Himself (10b). Many stage, screen and television productions demonstrate man's persistence in this attitude. James saw such men as little better than animals (12). The tragedy is that so many are led astray by their excesses.

Worst of all, such error leads to antinomianism. Unable to distinguish liberty from licence the teachers of whom Peter speaks offered their devotees the wrong kind of freedom (19), a word constantly misused in contemporary society. In reality such 'freedom' is only the pathway to a deeper bondage. It is a shock to learn that these false teachers had once had an experience of Christ (although some commentators understand them to have had only an intellectual appreciation of the gospel). No wonder Peter concludes that it would have been better for them never to have known the way, since they had now forsaken it (21). Such are the depths of sin into which even professing Christians may sink if they apostasize from the truth.

## Questions for further study and discussion on Studies 36-44

1. Is externalism restricted to the religious non-Christian today or may the true Christian be guilty of it?

2. What are the intellectual roads to salvation without God which are offered in the modern world?

3. Can you understand why the gospel has so often seemed antinomian to some of its critics? What other New Testament passages show clearly that it is not?

4. How far does Rom. 7.7–25 refer to Paul's experience before he became a Christian?

5. To what extent is sin the result of ignorance? Does ignorance excuse sin?

6. In what ways does the expression of sin vary from generation to generation?

7. What are the first questions I should ask of a man on the doorstep who wants to talk to me about religion?